C000142579

Cosmophobia Theory Mono
Standard Edition

Monograph 1

A SYNOPSIS

OF THE

COSMOPHOBIA THEORY

by

S.M.A. Malik

Sixth Edition

ROSENEATH SCIENTIFIC PUBLICATIONS

Roseneath Scientific Publications
Roseneath House, Brookside Crescent
Worcester Park, Surrey KT4 8AQ
Great Britain

Copyright © by S.M.A. Malik 1981, 1986, 1989, 1991, 1993, 1999, 2000

All rights reserved. Except for brief quotations by reviewers in journals or books, this publication, or parts thereof, must not be reproduced, stored in a retrieval system, or transmitted, in any form or by any means, electronic, mechanical, photocopying, or otherwise, without permission in writing from the publisher.

S.M.A. Malik: Cosmophobia Theory Monographs
Standard Fourth Edition
ISBN 1 85708 200 1 (complete set of 67 monographs)

Monograph 1. A Synopsis of the Cosmophobia Theory
ISBN 1 85708 201 X

First Edition (of this book)	1981
Second Edition (of this book)	1986
First Edition (Standard)	1991
Second Edition (Standard)	1993
Third Edition (Standard and Compact)	1999
Fourth Edition (Standard and Compact)	2000

Printed and published in Great Britain
by Roseneath Scientific Publications

CONTENTS

INTRODUCTION

01. The cosmophobia theory is a comprehensive psychological theory which correlates and explains all the salient phenomena of the human mind, both in the race, i.e. in the domain of sociology and social anthropology, and in the individual, i.e. in the domain of psychology and psychiatry. Such an endeavour is only possible if one has the courage to cross the boundaries between arbitrarily established scientific disciplines—not only the boundaries between 'sociology' and 'social anthropology' and between 'normal psychology' and 'psychiatry' (= pathological psychology, or psychological medicine) but also, and above all, the boundary between the social and the individual, or between the sociological and anthropological on the one hand and the psychological and the psychiatric on the other. For example, today students of psychiatry are taught that a false belief is a 'delusion' only if it fulfils three criteria: it is not true to fact; it cannot be corrected by an appeal to reason; and it is out of harmony with the individual's education and surroundings (Henderson and Gillespie). It is this third criterion—the reference to surroundings—that reduces the definition to absurdity. In effect it implies that a false belief is false only if it is held by an individual: if it is held by a whole group of people—a tribe, a nation, or mankind at large—it is no longer false or 'delusional' no matter how manifestly absurd it may be. Thus the psychiatrist is willing to accept as pathological whatever the society around him decrees to be abnormal; what the society around him holds as valid and even sacred, no matter how manifestly absurd it may be, must remain taboo to the psychiatrist who should 'mind his own business' and not question the absurdities and follies accepted as normal by the society in which he lives even if these in reality are so similar to those of the 'patients' referred to him for treatment. To give a single example, a psychiatrist in Western Europe today is quite prepared to accept that an individual is mentally ill with 'schizophrenia' because that individual believes that he can perform miracles, e.g. walk over water or put the midday sun back a few hours. However, the psychiatrist is not supposed to correlate these 'delusions' with the virtually identical beliefs which we were all taught in childhood, at home and at school, about religion and the miracles supposed to have taken place two thousand years ago. Can the psychiatrist who buries his head in the sand like this, as soon as the delusions of his patients touch on the equally absurd beliefs cherished by society as a whole, ever hope to discover the cause of 'schizophrenia'? Indeed psychiatrists have recently tried in vain to discover the cause of 'schizophrenia' in the laboratory—in abnormal metabolism and biochemistry—piously and naively oblivious of the all-too-obvious fact that the same 'delusions' expressed in 'schizophrenia' were not only held in an almost identical form by savages everywhere in the world but are indeed also held, though in a modified and slightly more refined form, by our own society in which these absurd beliefs form the very foundations of the institutions of religion, marriage, and government on which our civilization rests. Of course I am not stating a novel view in this respect: this has already been stated more than half a

1. A Synopsis of the Cosmophobia Theory

century ago by J.G. Frazer, the scientific pioneer who developed social anthropology into a refined system awaiting a theoretical foundation to explain the vast mass of factual material which he had collected and carefully classified in his monumental published work. Frazer's classification of the mental evolution of man into three stages, viz. the Age of Magic, the Age of Religion, and the Age of Science, is essentially identical with my classification of the mental development of both the race (phylopsychogenesis) and the individual (ontopsychogenesis) into the three stages of mental undifferentiation (prephobophronesia), cosmophobia (phobophronesia), and rational thought (postphobophronesia). This classification, while shedding a flood of light on the evolution (past, present, and future) of human civilization, is of fundamental importance to the psychologist and the psychiatrist in the understanding of mental phenomena, both normal and pathological, in individuals in our own society. In the last analysis, the psychologist and the psychiatrist on the one hand, and the sociologist and social anthropologist on the other, study two sides of the same field: that of the human mind and all it has created. The psychologist and the psychiatrist study the individual in great detail: they, as it were, study man under the microscope; whereas the sociologist and social anthropologist study societies consisting of hundreds, thousands, or millions of people, including mankind at large. What cannot be too strongly emphasized is that these two sides are complementary to each other and that neither of them can be understood without the other: there can be no psychiatry without sociology, and no sociology without psychiatry: without studying the race it is futile to try to understand the individual, and without studying the individual it is futile to try to understand the race. But having said that, we must remember that the race existed long before individuals in our society came about, so that there is no doubt about which of the two came first. It is quite true that the scientist sometimes has to work backwards—in this case use the study of the individual to shed light on the study of the race—but it is evident that the race is much older than the individual and that we should seek to understand the individual in terms of the race, and not the race in terms of the individual. For example, 'schizophrenia' may be said to reproduce, in a distorted atavistic form, the savagery of our remote primitive ancestors. But although the study of 'schizophrenia' in our own society may help elucidate many of the phenomena of savagery, savagery of course could not be said to reproduce 'schizophrenia'.

Hence, throughout the present study, all that is cultural, social, or sociological (the three terms are used more or less synonymously) is correlated with all that is individual or psychiatric (the two latter terms being used more or less synonymously, since 'psychiatry' in a broader sense comprises normal as well as pathological psychology).

02. That I have introduced a new nomenclature is purely incidental. The terms 'caustic soda', 'common salt', and 'Epsom salts' are unscientific: they do not indicate if these substances are simple compounds or are mixtures of compounds; they do not specify the chemical elements contained in each compound, and therefore do not show any qualitative or quantitative differences in the composition of these compounds. By contrast, the scientific terms 'sodium hydroxide', 'sodium chloride', and 'magnesium sulphate' concisely and accurately state the composition of each compound, so that by the adoption of this system one could tabulate all the compounds so far discovered and, from gaps in the table, perhaps even predict the

5

existence of compounds which hitherto had not been known. In the case of psychogenesis—leaving aside such entities of descriptive psychiatry as 'depression' and 'anxiety neurosis' which in reality cover, not one, but a variety of unrelated conditions—terms like 'palissymphronesia' (= atavistic mental undifferentiation, approximately the same entity as 'schizophrenia') and 'anancosymphronesia' (= stress mental undifferentiation, very approximately the same entity as 'hysteria') readily indicate the relation of these two conditions to other forms of normal and pathological 'symphronesia' (mental undifferentiation), e.g. in savages (prephobosymphronesia), in our own folklore and superstition (survival symphronesia or loiposymphronesia), and in certain vital functions such as language and thought (eusymphronesia). And of course symphronesia has its own place relative to other forms of mental orientation in the whole system of awareness. In this way a whole mass of apparently chaotic material—and this indeed covers all the main phenomena of sociology, social anthropology, psychology, and psychiatry—is brought within the compass of a single comprehensive psychological theory, each term in the new terminology of this system readily identifying the exact position of the condition concerned in the whole system. (Exceptions may be allowed, but should not be used too freely. For example, in chemistry it is usual to speak of 'water' rather than 'hydrogen oxide'; similarly, 'sadism' may be used in some cases instead of the rather cumbersome 'pragmophthorophilia'.)

03. I make no apologies for the use of the evolutionary approach. To have done otherwise would have been unscientific and hypocritical. For even though it is unfashionable nowadays to speak of 'savages' and 'backward nations', the euphemisms describing the same phenomena are freely used in everyday language: 'under-developed countries', 'countries of the Third World', etc. True savages have almost disappeared from the face of the earth, not because they were helped to civilization by their more advanced human brethren, but only because the lower savages were largely exterminated by the 'settlers' who usurped their land and often treated them like undesirable vermin, while the higher savages were too precious as chattels in the slave trade to exterminate, and were therefore severely exploited until they won their independence so that now they belong to the backward (but civilized) nations.

There is nothing unworthy in the fact that a nation is descended from savagery: all progressive nations must have passed through the stages of both savagery and backward civilization in their remote or recent history. Nor could savagery be a stigma for the savages who knew no better. Savagery is a stigma only if we cherish the delusion that we ourselves in the West are perfect. At present, the very writers who euphemistically refer to backward countries as the 'developing countries', frequently refer to the countries of the West as the 'developed countries': they are deluded enough to believe that we in the West are fully 'developed'. But in the eyes of posterity, as in the eyes of all the enlightened members of our own civilization today, we—far from being fully developed (if indeed there were such a thing)— are only barbarians who employ the cream of scientific knowledge to manufacture nuclear, chemical, bacteriological, and other weapons for the annihilation of fellow human beings. We are only witnessing the dawn of civilization, while still being torn by barbarism. That is why Tylor and Frazer approached the study of man with humility—humility which many contemporary anthropologists in Europe, and still more in America, view with sadistic contempt.

1. A Synopsis of the Cosmophobia Theory

The denial of cultural evolution by some sociologists and anthropologists is tantamount to admitting that man evolved from lower forms of animal life but that as soon as he became man—i.e. as soon as homo sapiens appeared on the face of the earth—evolution ceased and has been in abeyance ever since. This is so absurd scientifically that it could not be taken seriously. Besides, who can believe that, for example, the aborigines who occupied North America, and who in all the countless millennia of their existence had not even discovered the cultivation of crops or the domestication of animals, were at the same level of thought as the European settlers who—after exterminating these aborigines, who only had bows and arrows to defend themselves—built skyscrapers and aeroplanes, discovered nuclear energy, and invented computer technology?

In fact the study of savagery in the nineteenth and twentieth centuries largely followed the same pattern as the study of biology had done before it. In biology, scientists were at first struck by the differences between man and animals, man having the unique possession of thought and speech, but they later realized that, important as these differences were, the similarities between man and the other mammals were still greater—which ultimately led to the realization that man, far from having been created as a unique species, was in fact descended from lower forms of life. Similarly, in social anthropology, scientists were at first struck by the gulf between civilized man and primitive man who (at the lowest level of savagery) lived naked even in freezing temperatures, not having discovered the use of animal skins, and who, like other animals, lived by hunting and gathering. Only later, when the magical and animistic beliefs of savages were studied more fully, was it realized that the institutions of our own civilization were in fact deeply rooted in the crude and utterly irrational beliefs of savages. The inevitability of mankind outgrowing these crude institutions in the course of future evolution became obvious, and this was clearly stated by Frazer in cautious but unequivocal terms. This shocked fellow anthropologists and sociologists, who perhaps saw calling contemporary institutions into question as biting the hand that fed them. Ever since the publication of Psyche's Task, Frazer has been reviled by other anthropologists at every possible opportunity. But truth must eventually prevail. Our civilization, for all its technological progress, still rests on a foundation of barbarism. Men still worship imaginary beings in heaven while at the same time manufacture nuclear weapons to exterminate their fellow human beings. The 'schizophrenic' is a savage appearing atavistically in our midst; perhaps posterity, when true, rational civilization has at last been achieved, will regard the criminal who wants to exterminate fellow human beings as an atavistic reappearance of our present civilization.

Chapter 1

PHRONESIA

04. Human awareness (phronesia) can be studied in the race at various levels of civilization (phylopsychogenesis) and in the individual from earliest infancy onwards (ontopsychogenesis). The two studies are complementary and largely overlap, and the same terms are applied to both, any distinction necessary being rendered by the designation 'cultural' (or 'sociological', 'social', or 'racial') in the one case and 'individual' (or 'psychiatric') in the other. However, it is convenient to deal with the two separately as it is often easier to trace a particular mode of phronesic expression (i.e. a particular phronesic idiom) in one field than in the other. Mentally, as is the case physically, ontogenesis recapitulates phylogenesis: the development of the individual recapitulates the development of the race. Thus in both phylopsychogenesis and ontopsychogenesis we recognize three levels of mental evolution or development, which we refer to as the precosmophobic level of awareness, or prephobophronesia, the cosmophobic level of awareness, or phobophronesia, and the postcosmophobic level of awareness, or postphobophronesia. These levels, as well as their main subdivisions, are referred to as forms of phronesic (or mental) orientation, each of which comprises a number of phronesic idioms. The terms 'phronesic orientation' and 'phronesic idiom', representing major (or more general) and minor (or more special) forms or modes of phronesic expression respectively, are both used somewhat loosely within their own limits. For example, phagism as well as each of its three main divisions (viz. philism, sitism, and hectism) are all referred to as forms of phronesic orientation. Similarly, hydrism is an idiom and each of its subdivisions (hydrophilia, hydrolagnia, and hydrophobia) is also treated as an idiom. Occasionally the general characteristics of any form of phronesic orientation are referred to as general idioms (as distinct from specific idioms, which is the usual sense of the term); however, 'characteristics' is less ambiguous and is preferable to 'general idioms'. For example, such characteristics of scatism as autotropia and inanimatism may be referred to as general idioms of scatism.

The study of phronesic idioms, in cultures or in individuals, is referred to as idiomology. Thus, for example, the comparative study of different cultures as regards their phronesic idioms is referred to as 'comparative cultural idiomology'. Phronesiology is used in a wider sense: the study of human awareness (in general or in any of its aspects).

05. Prephobophronesia is the level of mental undifferentiation, or symphronesia, i.e. of man's relative mental undifferentiation from his environment, animate and inanimate, including fellow human beings. It is represented approximately by the stage of savagery (or primitive civilization) in the race, and by childhood in the case of the civilized individual. As there are other forms of mental undifferentiation, normal and pathological, to which we shall refer later, we speak of the symphronesia

8

1. A Synopsis of the Cosmophobia Theory

of prephobophronesia as <u>prephobophronesic symphronesia</u> or <u>prephobosymphronesia</u>. Prephobophronesia comprises prephobophronesic symphronesia (which is its main constituent) and the rudiments (if any) of cosmophobia, which we speak of as <u>rudimentary cosmophobia</u> or <u>archecosmophobia</u>, which differs from cosmophobia proper mainly in being unsystematized or poorly systematized (or unorganized or poorly organized).

Thus prephobophronesia is largely, but not entirely, synonymous with prephobosymphronesia, which is the ultimate prototype of all forms of symphronesia. Strictly speaking, however, although symphronesia is the essence of prephobophronesia, cosmophobia also does exist albeit in a rudimentary, unsystematized form. This is certainly true of phylopsychogenesis, as we do not know of any savages—when savages still existed in the world—who were free from rudimentary cosmophobia. But in ontopsychogenesis, it is a fact that the new-born infant—who shows his pleasure at sucking the breast and his displeasure by crying—does not show any evidence of psychological fear: he will let anyone hold him and he does not recognize his mother. Thus, during the early weeks (or few months) of life the infant may be assumed to be in a state of total prephobosymphronesia with no evidence of rudimentary cosmophobia.

The main manifestations of prephobophronesia are the belief in magic, including magical taboo, the belief in animism, collectivism or the collectivistic phenomena (the classificatory system of relationship, primitive group solidarity, etc.), and totemism. These are best studied in savages though they are also well represented in childhood, which from the psychogenetic point of view may be regarded as the recapitulation in ontogenesis of the stage of savagery in phylogenesis.

06. <u>Phobophronesia</u> is represented in the race by the stage of civilization proper (i.e. above the level of savagery or primitive civilization) as it has so far existed in history, and by the stages of adolescence and, to a lesser extent, adulthood in the individual. In it the symphronesia of earlier prephobophronesia gives way to the duality of two phronesic instincts: <u>hedonia</u> and <u>cosmophobia</u>. Hedonia is the search for, and gratification of, pleasure in the widest sense, including both physical and mental pleasure. Hedonia is deeply rooted in mental undifferentiation and its gratification is usually associated with the reinstatement, to a greater or lesser extent and in a temporary form, of prephobophronesic symphronesia—the most complete example being that of the rapture of orgasm which is as intense as it is short-lived. Cosmophobia is the irrational fear of the environment, animate and inanimate, including fellow human beings; the emphasis is on intellectual or ideational fear, though emotional fear is not excluded. Hedonia and cosmophobia have their origins in biological pleasure and biological fear, respectively. It should be emphasized, however, that although they include these biological instincts (or biological capacities for pleasure and fear), they are phronesic instincts and mainly represent the reflection in awareness of these biological instincts rather than the biological instincts themselves which, of course, existed in our animal ancestors long before the evolution of the human race. How the reflection in awareness of a biological instinct can alter the expression of that instinct is best illustrated by the case of homeroticism (or 'homosexuality') which transforms the biological instinct of sexuality, which is responsible for reproduction and the perpetuation of the race, into an asexual, sterile form that does not serve reproduction at all. Another example is that of destructiveness (phthorism), which is derived ultimately from the biological instinct

9

of consumptive feeding, and which, in the form of autophthorophilia (self-destructiveness) may lead the individual to suicide and therefore, instead of serving feeding and growth, serves self-annihilation.

Phobophronesia largely consists of biological awareness (biophronesia), i.e. awareness of the self and the environment in terms of the three main biological functions of alimentation (or feeding), excretion, and reproduction, the reflection in awareness of which gives rise to phagophronesia (or phagism), scatophronesia (or scatism), and erotophronesia (or eroticism), respectively. Each of these three main divisions has a hedonic and a cosmophobic form: thus, in the case of phagism, we have phagohedonia (which is synonymous with phagophilia) and phagocosmophobia (or phagophobia); in the case of scatism we have scatohedonia (comprising scatophilia and scatolagnia) and scatocosmophobia (or scatophobia); and in the case of eroticism we have eroticism and erotophobia. The main exception is in the case of neoscatism, which is subdivisible into protoscatism, which has a hedonic and a cosmophobic form, and deutoscatism, which has only a hedonic form. Biophronesia is not commensurate with phobophronesia for two reasons. On the one hand, prephobophronesia may be expressed in biophronesic terms as panphagism, a subject of some theoretical interest which is discussed in the monograph on The Oral Concept of the World. On the other hand, and much more importantly, the hedonic—but not the cosmophobic—forms of biophronesia survive into, and indeed form the essence of, postphobophronesia. (This does not apply to hedonic biophronesic idioms which are qualitatively dysphronesic or pathological, e.g. phthorophilia and dyseroticism in all their forms.)

There are two main differences between phagism and scatism. Phagism is allotropic, i.e. related mostly to the outside world, whereas scatism is autotropic, i.e. related mainly to the subject himself or herself. Also phagism is animatistic, i.e. related mostly to animate beings, real or imaginary (which includes the whole concept of animism, i.e. the belief in the soul whether this is supposed to be possessed by animate beings or by inanimate objects), whereas scatism is inanimatistic, i.e. is related mainly to inanimate (material or abstract) objects.

The main phylopsychogenetic manifestations of phobophronesia are the cardinal institutions of religion, marriage, and government, all of which are basically cosmophobic. By contrast, art is essentially hedonic even where its motivation is cosmophobic, e.g. in religious art.

07. Postphobophronesia is the stage representing the outgrowing, or conquest, of cosmophobia, and of those forms of hedonia which are antisocial (dyshedonia), e.g. sadism and other forms of phthorophilia, pleonexia in all its forms, and the various forms of dyseroticism. Postphobophronesia is essentially the stage of reason or rationalism whose four main idioms are: individualism, as against collectivism; materialism, as against animism; realism, as against subjectivity, arbitrariness, and cosmophobia; and rational (or social or postphobophronesic) morality, as against the prephobophronesic and phobophronesic forms of morality. In phylopsychogenesis, the postphobophronesic trend has been a regular characteristic of every progressive civilization, though its complete realization has never been attained. In ontopsychogenesis, it is represented—again in a partial form (i.e. in an admixture with phobophronesia)—by the maturity of adulthood. The main institutions of postphobophronesia are science, philosophy, and art. For although these latter exist in phobophronesic civilization, their position there is secondary

and they are wholly subservient to the primary phobophronesic institutions of religion, marriage, and government.

Having dealt briefly with the three stages of human mental evolution—prephobophronesia, phobophronesia, and postphobophronesia—it should be noted that we contrast symphronesia (which is the essential feature of prephobophronesia) with diaphronesia (= mental differentiation). Diaphronesia comprises the stages of phobophronesia and postphobophronesia as well as a certain pathological entity known as hyperphronesia (= mental overdifferentiation), a level of awareness at which hedonia is (usually only partially) outgrown (in much the same way as cosmophobia is outgrown in normal postphobophronesia), resulting in hyperphronesic anhedonia. (Thus hyperphronesia and hyperphronesic anhedonia are synonymous.)

Another point worth noting here is that although scatism generally represents a higher level of awareness than that of phagism, there are wide differences in phronesic level between the various forms of mental orientation, and between the various idioms within both phagism and scatism. Thus, within phagism, hectism represents a higher phronesic level than that of philism; and, within hectism, pleonexia represents a higher phronesic level than that of meionexia, and euexia represents a higher phronesic level than that of pleonexia. Within scatism, deutoscatism represents a higher phronesic level than that of protoscatism; and neoscatism as a whole (= protoscatism + deutoscatism) represents a higher phronesic level than that of palaeoscatism. Hence, within biophronesia, the widest difference in awareness between any two forms of mental orientation is that between philism and deutoscatism. Philism, because of its proximity in the phronesic scale to prephobosymphronesia, in which the ultimate essence of hedonia lies, is indispensable to life—which is particularly true of idiophilia, the central idiom of philism.

08. Now we can deal with the subject of euphronesia and dysphronesia, i.e. of normal and pathological thought, respectively, by the objective, rational standards of postphobophronesia. It will be evident that prephobosymphronesia is 'normal' for the savage, but its atavistic reappearance in civilization constitutes a serious mental disease, viz. palissymphronesia. Similarly, pleonexia and sadism are, on the whole, 'normal' in our phobophronesic civilization. Such 'normality' is only relative, and is therefore always written between inverted commas: it is not euphronesic since the latter refers to the absolute standards of postphobophronesia, by which prephobosymphronesia, pleonexia, and sadism are pathological, i.e. dysphronesic. More about this later.

09. Phagism is phylogenetically and ontogenetically older than scatism and eroticism; i.e. the alimentary function impresses itself on awareness long before the excretory and the reproductive functions do so. In fact scatism and eroticism, and their various idioms, are all modelled on, or are ultimately derived from, earlier phagistic prototypes. Thus in dealing with scatism and eroticism and their idioms we often refer to their phagistic basis, or phagobasis. For example, phthorism, which is a scatistic idiom, represents (in an ideal form) the reduction of objects to worthlessness with excreta, the latter being the prototype of all worthlessness and are therefore credited with having tremendous destructive powers; i.e. excreta, being themselves worthless, reduce everything they come into contact with to similarly worthless excreta. However, on a deeper plane, we can see that phthorism is derived

from, or is an excretory modification of, the phronesically earlier concept of consumptive devouring, which relates to alimentation and is therefore phagistic. In other words, phthorism has its phagobasis in consumptive devouring. We shall see other examples of phagobasis later.

10. Next we turn to terminology. Generally speaking, typically in scatism (for reasons that will be mentioned later), we use the suffix '-ism' to indicate an idiom, the non-erotic hedonic form of which is given the terminal element '-philia' while the cosmophobic form is given the terminal element '-phobia'. The erotic form, which of course is also hedonic, has the terminal element '-lagnia', and its cosmophobic form the terminal element '-lagnophobia'. The terminal element '-hedonia' covers both the non-erotic (-philia) and erotic (-lagnia) forms. Thus 'hydrism' is the idiom of water, of which 'hydrophilia' (= love of water) is the non-erotic hedonic form, while 'hydrophobia' (= fear of water) is the cosmophobic form. 'Hydrolagnia' (= erotic hydrophilia) is the erotic interest in water. 'Hydrohedonia' is a collective term for both hedonic forms, viz. hydrophilia and hydrolagnia: alternatively, we may speak of 'hydrophilia, non-erotic and erotic'. Similarly, 'phthorism' is the idiom of destructiveness. Its non-erotic hedonic form ('phthorophilia') is subdivisible into the active love of destructiveness ('pragmophthorophilia' or 'sadism'), the passive love of destructiveness, i.e. the love of being destroyed ('apragmophthorophilia' or 'masochism'), and self-destructiveness ('autophthorophilia'). The corresponding erotic forms are 'pragmophthorolagnia' or 'erotic sadism', 'apragmophthorolagnia' or 'erotic masochism', and 'autophthorolagnia'. The cosmophobic form may be non-erotic ('phthorophobia') or erotic ('phthorolagnophobia' or 'erotic phthorophobia').

It should be noted here that for an idiom with the termination '-ism' the adjective always has the ending '-istic'. The simple adjectival termination '-ic' has no specific relation to any particular idiom. For example, 'kinetistic' means 'of, or pertaining to, kinetism'; by contrast, 'kinetic' simply means 'related to movement', and so 'kinetic' may refer to agility, kinetism, or myotonophilia, which are three different idioms, or indeed it may refer to movement in any sense whatsoever.

Some idioms have no cosmophobic forms, or doubtful ones, in which case—especially where the root word is long—the termination '-philia' may be omitted. This omission, however, invites ambiguity and should not, therefore, be used too liberally. For example, in deutoscatism (which has no cosmophobic forms), 'monosynthesis', 'protophasia', and 'deutophasia' are used in preference to 'monosyntheticophilia', 'protophasiophilia', and 'deutophasiophilia'.

Normal (i.e. euphronesic) variations in euphronesic, and therefore necessarily hedonic, idioms are indicated by the prefix 'poly-' for the presence of an idiom to a marked degree, and 'oligo-' (or 'olig-') for its presence to a slight degree. By contrast, the presence of an idiom to a pathologically (i.e. dysphronesically) excessive degree (with or without a simultaneous qualitative change) is indicated by the prefix 'hyper-' or, occasionally, 'pleo-' (or 'pleon-'); decrease or impairment of an idiom to a dysphronesic degree is indicated by the prefix 'hypo-' (or 'hyp-'). Thus 'polyphilophilia', 'oligophilophilia', 'polyeroticism', and 'oligeroticism' are all euphronesic conditions that refer to normal, cultural or individual, variations in philophilia and eroticism. (Of course the prefix 'poly-' in 'polygamy' and 'polyandry' is not attached to a hedonic idiom, and therefore has no implication of euphronesic hedonic abundance.) By contrast, 'hyperphilophilia', 'hypereroticism',

1. A Synopsis of the Cosmophobia Theory

and 'pleonexia' all refer to pathological excessiveness, while 'hypositophilia' and 'hyporgastia' indicate pathological (i.e. dysphronesic) reduction. The prefix 'a-' (or 'an-') is used in word-formation in a variety of ways (by no means limited to hedonic idioms), to indicate either absence or reduction, either in a euphronesic sense (e.g. 'atheism', 'agamy', and 'acracy') or in a dysphronesic sense (e.g. 'aneroticism' and 'anorgastia'). 'Anhedonic anhedonia' (i.e. anhedonia due to actual hedonic loss) is essentially euphronesic, though it is usual for it in phobophronesic civilization to have dysphronesic complications.

The prefixes 'eu-' and 'dys-' are used to indicate the normal and the pathological respectively—normality and pathogenicity being invariably meant in the absolute, postphobophronesic sense of euphronesia and dysphronesia referred to earlier. Where 'normality' refers not to true euphronesia but is merely relative to the standards of a stage of mental evolution other than postphobophronesia (viz. either prephobophronesia or phobophronesia), it is always distinguished by being written between inverted commas. It is worth noting that whereas all cosmophobic idioms are dysphronesic, not all hedonic idioms are euphronesic. For although hedonia in general is euphronesic, there are important exceptions, notably palaeoscatophilia in all its forms (phthorophilia, propetophilia, and skoroidophilia), all forms of dyseroticism, and all pathologically exaggerated forms (the hyper- or pleo-forms) of otherwise normal hedonic idioms: these are the main forms of dyshedonia. Thus—qualitatively dysphronesic hedonic idioms apart—the dysphronesic form of an idiom generally includes both its cosmophobic form and its hyper- or pleo-form. For example, in 'hectism' we contrast 'euexia' (= euhectophilia) with 'dyshectism' which includes aphormic hectophobia, 'meionexia' (= stratificatory hectophobia), and 'pleonexia' (= stratificatory pleohectophilia).

Wherever '-eroticism' occurs as a terminal element, '-lagnia' may be substituted; e.g. 'auteroticism' = 'autolagnia' and 'homeroticism' = 'homolagnia' (short for 'homogeneroticism' and 'homogeneolagnia' respectively).

We use '-poeic' to indicate 'producing' or 'giving rise to', in contrast to '-genic', which means 'arising from'. (The current use in medicine of '-genic' for both opposite senses is deplorable.)

'Civilization' and 'culture' are used completely synonymously. 'Savagery' and 'primitive civilization' are synonymous, and are contrasted with 'civilization proper'.

Chapter 2

SYMPHRONESIA

11. The prephobosymphronesia of savagery partially survives in phobophronesic civilization in the form of superstition, folklore, etc., thus giving rise to survival symphronesia (loiposymphronesia). Loiposymphronesia is thus essentially a milder, or diluted, form of prephobosymphronesia. Prephobosymphronesia also occurs in civilization in two modified forms, one of which (stress symphronesia or anancosymphronesia) is benign, not unrelated to survival symphronesia, and is usually precipitated in predisposed individuals by stress of some kind; the other (reversion (or atavistic) symphronesia or palissymphronesia) is malignant inasmuch as it represents mental reversion of a civilized individual to savagery, in a partial, distorted, garbled, and useless or harmful form, for he is neither a 'normal' savage at the prephobophronesic level nor a 'normal' civilized person at the phobophronesic level. Quite apart from all these dysphronesic forms, i.e. all these forms of dyssymphronesia, symphronesia (in the form of eusymphronesia or essential symphronesia) forms the basis of such essential mental functions as hedonia, biophronesia, language, and indeed the very process of thinking which, like language, is symbolic and therefore rests on the equation, or undifferentiation, of two objects, e.g. a word and a concept in the case of language or mental images and reality in the case of thinking.

12. As for prephobosymphronesia, which is the prototype of all symphronesia, and which is approximately commensurate with the stage of savagery in the mental evolution of the race, this rests ultimately on the relative lack or absence of the concepts of space and time. This explains, among other things, the belief in the possible ubiquity (or omnipresence) and eternity of man, and in the possibility of knowing the distant past and the future (and so of prophesying the future) since the distinction between past, present, and future is, in one sense, obliterated or, rather, not yet established. The relative absence of the space and time concepts also explains the belief in the possible mutability of natural law, which is known at higher levels of awareness to be immutable. Hence the essential belief that 'all is possible' and that the phenomena of nature can be altered, at any rate by clever or powerful magicians, which produces what at higher levels of awareness is referred to as 'miracles'. All these manifestations form the very essence of the belief in magic. We have already referred to some examples (prophesying, miracles, etc.); others include the belief in telepathy and in magical telescopy ('clairvoyance') and magical telephony, which are examples of the belief in the possibility of omnipresence of a person.

By subjectivity and arbitrariness we mean, respectively, the savage's conception of the world in terms of himself, and the holding of beliefs unsupported by reality.

Another important manifestation of prephobosymphronesia, which ultimately must be due to the relative lack of the space and time concepts, is that of the confusion of subject and object, of different objects in the environment, and of thought (especially wish or fear) with reality. Totemism is an example of the confusion of subject and object, whereas the collectivistic phenomena, including the classificatory system of relationship, are mainly examples of the confusion of different objects in the environment, in this case similarity being equated with identity. The confusion of wish and fear with reality is best exemplified by the savage who, believing that the spear that had wounded him was charmed, lay down and refused food till he died. It is evident that savages in general, and the loiposymphronesic ignorant classes in phobophronesic civilization, are credulous and 'suggestible', especially when it comes to sensitive matters of wish or fear.

13. Anancosymphronesia is closely related to the 'normal' prephobosymphronesia of savagery and its survival in the ignorant classes in phobophronesic civilization in the form of loiposymphronesia. In these essentially prephobophronesic groups, anancosymphronesia simply represents a certain intensification of prephobosymphronesia under the influence of stress. Thus the savage referred to earlier who, believing that the spear that had wounded him was charmed and therefore lethal, lay down and pined away, may be described as an anancosymphronesic. The main difference between anancosymphronesia and 'normal' prephobosymphronesia (in savages or as loiposymphronesia in civilization) is that anancosymphronesia is precipitated by stress—which is true even of the less common cases among the enlightened and well-educated. The type of stress precipitating the illness (in predisposed individuals) ranges from general discontent with life, or unhappiness arising primarily from cultural or individual circumstances, to androphobia, aphilia, and legal crises. The main symphronesic manifestations encountered in the illness are the materialization of discontent, which is a form of the materialization of the abstract, and the confusion of thought (wish and fear) with reality. However, any of the other manifestations of prephobosymphronesia may also be encountered.

14. In contrast to anancosymphronesia, palissymphronesia is essentially a malignant condition. For anancosymphronesia is essentially adaptive and benign; even though its adaptation to stress is often like that of the ostrich that buries its head in the sand, and although rarely it may end fatally (e.g. in the sitandrophobic woman who starves herself, or in the savage who did the same because he believed he had been wounded by a charmed spear), it does not usually completely alienate the patient from reality. By contrast, in most cases palissymphronesia swamps the patient mentally with a garbled version of prephobosymphronesia that is completely out of context in present-day life, which renders him incapable of work, of fending for himself, or of living a useful life in any way. However, there is a basic connection between the two conditions since they both represent special forms of prephobosymphronesia. Undoubtedly many cases which receive the label anancosymphronesia, or even perfectly 'normal' loiposymphronesia, in the ignorant and illiterate classes, would be labelled palissymphronesia if seen in educated, intelligent individuals. For example, a peasant in a remote rural area who believes that a local monument is haunted may be expressing 'normal' loiposymphronesia; the same belief in a university graduate in a city would suggest palissymphronesia.

The manifestations (or 'symptoms') of palissymphronesia are essentially those of savage prephobosymphronesia, except that they present in a patchy and distorted form, as might be expected from such a reversion (or atavistic) disorder. Thus they are best classified in terms of savage institutions as magical, animistic, collectivistic, and totemistic symptoms (or delusions, since they are false beliefs, remembering always that this applies equally to beliefs held by the race as a whole at the prephobophronesic and phobophronesic levels of cultural evolution). To these may be added cosmophobic delusions and synhedonia. Such phenomena as subjectivity, arbitrariness, and the incapacity for abstract thought are commonly seen in the palissymphronesic as they are in the savage. Magical delusions include, inter alia, such special forms as telepathy, magical telescopy, magical telephony, and magical taboo (in association with archecosmophobia). Animistic delusions include mythological and religious delusions. What is descriptively termed 'hallucinations' (false sensory perceptions) most often arises from the magical delusions (e.g. hearing people at a distance (magical telephony)) or from animistic belief (e.g. hearing the voices of invisible people—of what in effect are spirits or ghosts). Synhedonia is of special interest as it has no equivalent in savagery. It is a manifestation of the malignancy of the reversion form of symphronesia (i.e. of palissymphronesia) as against the 'normal' symphronesia of savagery. Synhedonia is mainly a disorder of emotion resulting from the palissymphronesic loss of the polarity (or duality) of subject and hedonic object. The condition is most often manifested as apathy, i.e. loss of the capacity for all emotional experience, e.g. for both joy and sadness, but sometimes there may be other forms of emotional abnormality, e.g. depression, elation, or emotional incongruity. Both the ability to work and eroticism may also be severely affected. Occasionally synhedonia is the main manifestation of palissymphronesia (synhedonic palissymphronesia (the 'simple schizophrenia' of descriptive psychiatry), which is an arrested form of the disease, in contrast to symphronesic palissymphronesia, which is the fully-developed, and more typical, form of the disease).

Chapter 3

PHAGISM

15. Phagophronesia, or phagism for short, is subdivisible into three main forms of phronesic orientation: philism, sitism, and hectism. Philism rests on a basis of preservative devouring, i.e. devouring that unites two individuals without one of them consuming the other as is the case with consumptive devouring, which is the basis of hectism. Preservative devouring has its biological origin in earliest infancy, in which the infant feeds at—or, to be more precise, on—the breast without ever consuming it. Philism is therefore ontogenetically and phylogenetically older than hectism. Both sitism and hectism have their biological basis, not in the lactivorous stage of life like philism, but in the later omnivorous stage of consumptive devouring, of which the most important aspect is the carnivorous aspect in which one being feeds on the flesh of another so that life is maintained only at the expense of other lives. The main difference between the two is that sitism is concrete whereas hectism is ideal.

Philism rests on the equation of food (or aliment) with love: to devour or be devoured preservatively is to love or be loved. The equivalent basis of hectism is the equation of food with property, the property may be human or non-human. Thus, in hectism, to devour is to own (material objects or fellow human beings). Finally, in sitism food remains as food: it is not equated with anything else.

16. First we consider philism. Philism has a hedonic form (philophilia) and a cosmophobic form (philophobia or, as we generally prefer to call it, aphilia). However, in philism the hedonic form definitely predominates: the cosmophobic form represents a reduction in, or an abatement of, the hedonic form rather than the transformation of pleasure into fear. (By contrast, in hectism, especially when we consider the importance of aphormic hectophobia, cosmophobia is more important than hedonia.) Hence, with one main exception, viz. anidiophilia, we have no special names for the cosmophobic forms of individual philophilic idioms: we group them all together under the term 'aphilia', for they are in reality the same hedonic idioms only in a reduced form.

17. The idioms of philophilia are: idiophilia, optimism, gaiety, love of decoration, agility, generosity and hospitality, gregariousness, familiarity, uninhibitedness, emotional expressiveness (including artistic expressiveness), volubility and linguistic ability (phatophilia), and love of singing (odophilia). Only idiophilia requires special treatment here.

18. Idiophilia is the central idiom of philophilia—the one from which all the others are derived; hence we refer to all the idioms of philophilia apart from idiophilia as the associated idioms of idiophilia. By idiophilia we mean love proper, i.e. a sense of belonging to another person, or an emotional bond between two persons, of the opposite or of the same sex. The ontogenetic prototype of idiophilia is the child's love for the mother, more specifically for her breast as it is equated with

17

food or aliment, or (to put it more precisely) for the mother as she is equated with her breast and with food or aliment. The mother we mean here is, of course, the racial mother, or instinctual mother, and not the individual mother, though the latter is included in the racial mother. This explains why many individuals who were never neglected by their mothers go through life with ineradicable aphilia, while many others who were neglected and badly treated by their mothers go through life with exuberant philophilia. For philophilia, like virtually all other idioms in the individual, is mainly determined by heredity: environmental factors can aggravate or moderate the hereditary predisposition (in the case of dysphronesic idioms), but there is no doubt whatever that heredity is the main determining factor.

Idiophilia is the prototype of all hedonia. Since the prototype of idiophilia itself is the love of the mother, all hedonia may be said to ultimately represent metrophilia (= love of the mother) or, since the mother is equated with her breast, to represent mastometrophilia (= love of the mother's breast). However, we should remember that hedonia as the love of the mother represents a desire, not for union with the mother, but rather for reunion with her, viz. for reinstating (in a temporary and illusory form) the oro-mammary relation that united the child with the mother (or her breast) at the prephobophronesic stage of ontogenetic development. Hence metrophilia as the ultimate prototype of all hedonia is more accurately described as metropalinodophilia (= desire for mother-reunion or mother-reversion).

Similarly, the cosmophobic equivalent of idiophilia, viz. anidiophilia (the sense of unlovedness or unwantedness or rejectedness) is the central idiom of aphilia, and is the prototype of all cosmophobia.

19. We need not here trace the development of hedonia and cosmophobia from idiophilia (ultimately in relation to the mother, i.e. metrophilia) and anidiophilia, respectively, but some of the more important manifestations and derivatives of these philistic idioms, and some of the scatistic and erotic idioms for which these philistic idioms are the phagobasis, should be noted. To begin with, there is geneosemeiophilia, which is a special form of idiophilia representing interest in the representation in awareness of the characteristics of the two sexes, in the non-erotic sense. We have noted that idiophilia represents love of fellow human beings of both sexes; geneosemeiophilia represents the sexual aspect (in the non-erotic sense) of this love of, or interest in, both sexes, i.e. interest in people, not as sexless individuals, but as men and women. Geneosemeiophilia is an integral part of idiophilia. By contrast, autophilia (= self-love) is a derivative of metrophilia in which metrophilia, i.e. idiophilia in relation to the mother, is partly replaced by self-love: love of oneself partly serves as a temporary substitute for love of the mother. Thus autophilia is, strictly speaking, a derivative of idiophilia, more precisely a derivative of the prototype of idiophilia, viz. idiophilia in relation to the mother (which is what metrophilia is). Thus when we say that idiophilia is the prototype of all hedonia, this applies also to autophilia and to the whole of scatism that is derived from it.

Autophilia is the basis of all scatism and gives it its characteristic autotropia and inanimatism, whereas idiophilia, from its prototype in metrophilia, continues to be the basis of all phagism and gives it its characteristic allotropia and animatism. Thus allotropia and animatism are ontogenetically older than autotropia and inanimatism, and the same is true phylogenetically: phagism is phylogenetically older than scatism.

1. A Synopsis of the Cosmophobia Theory

Apart from the fact that phagism is derived from idiophilia whereas scatism is derived from autophilia (which itself is ultimately also derived from idiophilia), there is the fact that <u>normal eroticism</u> (<u>eueroticism</u>) rests on a phagobasis of idiophilia, whereas most serious forms of <u>dyseroticism</u> are derived from autophilia.

On the other hand, anidiophilia (or, put more generally, aphilia) is the phagobasis of all <u>phthorism</u> (sadism, masochism, autophthorophilia, and phthorophobia). An interesting aspect of aphilia is that, like some other cosmophobic idioms, it is 'normal' at the phobophronesic level of civilization (except in its extreme forms). Moreover, being philistic, it is commoner in polyphilic (i.e. predominantly philophilic) than in polyneoscatistic (i.e. predominantly neoscatistic) civilizations; and, being cosmophobic, it is commoner in backward than in progressive civilizations. Aphilia may undergo a complication in which the sense of unlovedness (anidiophilia) is replaced by a sense of overlovedness (<u>hyperidiophilia</u>), thus giving rise to a condition known as <u>hyperphilophilia</u> (or <u>hyperphilia</u>). Hyperphilia is invariably secondary to aphilia. In other words, whereas in the case of hectism pleonexia is most often (though not always) a primary condition (i.e. is not secondary to meionexia), in the case of philism hyperphilia is always secondary to aphilia (though this aphilia may be mild or moderate enough to be regarded as 'normal' at the phobophronesic level of civilization, or it may be so severe as to be regarded as pathological even at the phobophronesic level). Hyperphilia, though to a much lesser extent than aphilia, is also regarded in its milder forms as 'normal' at the phobophronesic level of civilization. In some cases a patient may oscillate irregularly between severe aphilia and severe hyperphilia, with or without periods of relative normality between the aphilic and the hyperphilic phases—a condition to which we refer as <u>amphiphilia</u>. Severe aphilia, either on its own or alternating with severe hyperphilia (i.e. as part of amphiphilia), may have <u>deutoscatistic complications</u>. Thus aphilia may be complicated by a pathologically exaggerated first deutoscatistic phase (hyperprotophasia), usually in the form of either autophthorophilia or sphalerohedonia, or a combination of both. Similarly, hyperphilia in cases of amphiphilia may be complicated by a pathologically excessive second deutoscatistic phase (hyperdeutophasia), e.g. in the form of hypererasophilia. These deutoscatistic conditions will be referred to in the chapter on scatism.

Normal philophilia, in the postphobophronesic sense, is referred to as <u>euphilophilia</u> (or <u>euphilia</u>). Thus <u>dysphilism</u> comprises aphilia and hyperphilia (and amphiphilia).

Finally, the reader will no doubt have noted that because of the duplication of the 'phil-' element in 'philophilia', whenever a prefix is added to this word the first element—the '-philo-' part—may be omitted to shorten the word. Thus we generally use the shortened forms 'euphilia', 'aphilia', 'polyphilia', and 'hyperphilia' instead of the longer forms 'euphilophilia', 'aphilophilia', 'polyphilophilia', and 'hyperphilophilia'.

Before we leave the subject of philism we have to elaborate a little on geneosemeism. The sexual characteristics represented in geneosemeism may be either general, i.e. relating to the general configuration and other general characteristics of the human male and female body, or special, i.e. relating to the configuration and other (scopic, haptic, and ideal, etc.) characteristics of specifically male or specifically female organs, of which the most important are the breasts and the womb (= anatomical vagina and uterus) in the woman (<u>mastosemeism</u> and hysterosemeism) and the penis in the man (phallosemeism). We often speak of the sexual characteristics concerned as geneoids, which comprise gynoids (including mastoids and hysteroids), androids (including phalloids), and mixoids. Regarding general geneosemeism, the most outstanding fact about the general physical configuration of the sexes is that men are relatively tall but thin while women are relatively short but plump. Hence the androsemeism of verticality (orthism) and upward-pointing (anatropism), and the gynosemeism of horizontality (epipedism) and downward-pointing (catatropism). The main idioms of mastosemeism are: prosthekism (decorative appendages of all kinds conceived as mastoid appendages), leiism (smoothness that is associated with softness), malakism (softness), sphericism (roundness or sphericity), leukism (the colour white, in this case mastoleukism, as distinct from hydroleukism), catatropism, and artiarithmism (even, as opposed to odd, numbers). The main idioms of hysterosemeism are hollowness, penetrability (or receptivity), fertility (or fecundity), and enterythrism (the colour red in relation to the interior of the body, viz. the mucous membranes of such cavities as the mouth and the vagina). Finally, the main idioms of phallosemeism are: xestism (smoothness in association with hardness), sclerism (hardness), oxyism (angularity or pointedness), anatropism, penetrativeness, melanism (the colour black), rhabdophalloidism (rod-like phalloids), and perissarithmism (odd, as against even, numbers). It should be noted that some idioms, e.g. catatropism and anatropism, are common to both general and special geneosemeism. Another important point to note is that most (but not all) gynoids (including mastoids and hysteroids) are also hydroids, while most androids (including phalloids) are also stereoids. Moreover, generally speaking, hydroids have gynosemeistic associations whereas stereoids have androsemeistic associations. Of special importance here is the equation in awareness 'man = penis = solid matter = stereoid' and 'woman = womb = hollow = space = hydroid'. Thus, on the basis of the equation of the man with his penis and the woman with her womb, the man is the stereoid that fills the hydroid hollow of the woman in coitus.

20. Next we turn to sitism. Of the three main forms of phronesic orientation in phagism, sitism is the most concrete. Sitism is much more closely related to philism than to hectism for two reasons: like philism, sitism is predominantly hedonic; and philism and sitism represent a lower level of awareness than that of hectism.

Sitophilia shows wide cultural and individual variations. Generally speaking, it correlates with philophilia so that polyphilic cultures and individuals tend to be the polysitophilic cultures and individuals, while oligophilic (e.g. polydeutoscatistic, especially polyprotophasic) cultures and individuals tend to be the oligositophilic cultures and individuals.

Normal anhedonic anhedonia (i.e. anhedonia resulting from actual hedonic loss) may cause a general impairment of hedonia, including oligositophilia. However, at the phobophronesic level of civilization, anhedonic anhedonia is commonly conceived (at least partly) in aphilic terms and this aphilia (in so far as sitism is concerned) may result in either hypositophilia or compensatory hypersitophilia. Aphilia is also the basis of sitophobia. Clinically, sitophobia is most often secondary to androphobia—a condition to which we refer as sitophobic androphobia or sitandrophobia. Strictly speaking, sitandrophobia is a special form of androphobic anancosymphronesia in which the androphobia presents in the form of sitophobia. Like androphobic anancosymphronesia in general, sitandrophobia

1. A Synopsis of the Cosmophobia Theory

is most often seen in young women and occasionally in homandrolagnic men.

21. Finally we deal with hectism. In hectism—culturally the most important division of phagism at the phobophronesic level of civilization—food is equated with property or ownership, i.e. the ownership of fellow human beings or of the non-human environment. It is on this distinction between human and non-human ownership that the distinction between dyshectism and euexia depends. In religion and marriage the ownership is strictly human; in government, non-human ownership—as long as it is private—proves ultimately to be essentially a form of human ownership, since what matters is not the non-human objects themselves that are owned but the fact that they represent the necessaries, comforts, and luxuries of life so that their private ownership by a minority of individuals excludes the majority from their enjoyment, and so reduces that majority to a subject class, and so to being in effect (partly if not fully) owned as human property by the individuals who own the non-human objects. Thus euexia applies only to non-human property that is fully socially owned, i.e. owned by mankind as a whole.

22. Hectism is subdivisible into animistic hectism, represented by the institution of religion; sexual hectism, represented by the institution of marriage and its corollary, the family; and practical hectism, represented in the euphronesic form by euexia, and in the dysphronesic form by the institution of government or politics (in the widest sense, the two terms being used synonymously). In each of these divisions the essence of the phobophronesic institution concerned lies in a special form of cosmophobia which we call aphormic hectophobia, or simply aphormic cosmophobia. Thus aphormic animistic hectophobia or cosmophobia is represented by the fear, and so the worship, of supernatural beings or 'gods'. Aphormic sexual hectophobia or cosmophobia is represented by the fear of the womb, especially of one's own mother's womb (kyemetrophobia), and so by the fear and prohibition of 'incest', represented primarily by the mother incest taboo. Aphormic practical hectophobia or cosmophobia is represented by the fear of unorthodoxy (of thought and behaviour) in the widest sense (anorthodoxophobia), which gives rise to the rules that enforce conformity in phobophronesic society—the unwritten rules of custom and tradition, and written legal codes that are usually ultimately derived from custom and tradition.

In addition to aphormic hectophobia there is stratificatory hectism, viz. hedonic, represented by the pleonexia (i.e. pleohectophilia) of the upper class in each of the three cardinal institutions mentioned above; and cosmophobic, represented by the meionexia (i.e. stratificatory hectophobia) of the lower class in each institution. In the study of phobophronesia we usually find that pleonexia is generally associated with a greater or lesser degree of sadism, and that meionexia is generally associated with a greater or lesser degree of phthorophobia. In this association of hectism with phthorism in phobophronesia, hectism is usually of primary importance while phthorism is of secondary importance. Thus, both in the study of culture and in the study of the individual, we often speak of phthoristic-dyshectistic phobophronesia (or phthoristic dyshectism), which comprises sadistic-pleonectic phobophronesia, or sadistic pleonexia, and phthorophobic-meionectic phobophronesia, or phthorophobic meionexia. For example, in social stratification (religious, sexual, and political) the upper classes are the sadistic-pleonectic classes while the lower classes are the phthorophobic-meionectic classes.

Finally, as noted above, euexia (i.e. euhectophilia) is not only limited to practical hectism but is specifically limited to non-human property that is fully socially owned, i.e. owned by mankind as a whole.

23. Closely related to hectophobia is <u>aetheophobia</u>, i.e. fear of the unusual, strange, 'unnatural', incomprehensible, or novel. Aetheophobia is all-pervasive in cosmophobia, and may be seen in the archecosmophobia of savagery, and its survival or recurrence in loiposymphronesia and palissymphronesia in civilization, as well as in the cosmophobia proper of phobophronesic civilization, in which (among other things) it is closely related to all three forms (animistic, sexual, and practical) of aphormic hectophobia. <u>Aetherotophobia</u> and <u>aetheomorphophobia</u> are special forms of aetheophobia in relation, respectively, to unusual or 'unnatural' forms of eroticism (whether these are in reality euerotic or dyserotic) and to disfigured persons and objects.

Chapter 4

SCATISM

24. <u>Scatism</u> is the reflection in awareness of the excretory functions of urination and defaecation. Scatohedonia cannot normally exist to the exclusion of phagohedonia, whose prototype is idiophilia—but phagohedonia can exist without scatohedonia. Hence we refer to phagohedonia as <u>protohedonia</u>, which particularly applies to philophilia (more specifically to idiophilia), while scatohedonia is referred to as <u>deutohedonia</u>. (Normal eroticism also belongs to protohedonia: it essentially represents a special form of idiophilia.) This distinction between the two forms of hedonia is particularly important in sphalerohedonia and autophthorophilia.

We divide scatism into <u>palaeoscatism</u> and <u>neoscatism</u>. Neoscatism in turn is divided into <u>protoscatism</u> and <u>deutoscatism</u>.

25. <u>Palaeoscatism</u> comprises four main idioms: skoroidism, phthorism, propetism, and shame. It is the lowest, or most archaic, division of scatism: it represents the concept of excreta as a worthless, and so by implication as a highly destructive, product, i.e. not only are excreta worthless but they also reduce to worthlessness (i.e. destroy) everything they (concretely or ideally) come into contact with. Hence the fact that palaeoscatism, even in its hedonic forms, is not adapted to rational civilization, and is therefore antisocial and dysphronesic in its entirety. Because palaeoscatism is dysphronesic in its entirety, its hedonic idioms do not take the prefixes 'poly-', 'hyper-', 'oligo-', and 'hypo-'.

<u>Skoroidism</u> is the central idiom of palaeoscatism from which the other idioms are derived. It represents pleasure and fear in relation to excreta and (concrete or ideal) excreta-like objects, e.g. foul odour and dirtiness, and in relation to excretory acts where these acts involve other people, viz. excretory acts in other people and the subject's own excretory acts if they involve other people. This last point, viz. the involvement of other people in excretory acts, is important in the distinction between skoroidism and skoreticism: the latter is a neoscatistic idiom to which we shall refer later. Here we should note that skoroidism comprises <u>coproidism</u> in relation to faeces and (concrete or ideal) faeces-like objects and defaecation involving others, and <u>uroidism</u> in relation to urine and urine-like objects and urination involving others. The central idiom of coproidism is <u>coprism</u> (in relation to faeces themselves and defaecation involving others); similarly the central idiom of uroidism is <u>urism</u> (in relation to urine itself and urination involving others). Other idioms of skoroidism include <u>mysism</u> (interest in, and fear of, dirt and dirtiness), of which mysolalism (in relation to 'dirty' or 'obscene' language) is a special ideal form, and <u>skoroborism</u> (the eating of excreta, comprising coproborism and uroborism), and <u>mysoborism</u> (the eating of dirt). Finally, sensory perception in relation to skoroidism is referred to as <u>skoroidaestheticism,</u> which is an idiom of skoroidism, and therefore of palaeoscatism, and which should not be confused with aestheticism, which is a neoscatistic idiom. In relation to excreta themselves, skoraestheticism (comprising

23

copraestheticism and uraestheticism) comprises skorosphreticism, skorohapticism, skoracousticism, skoroscopism, and skorogeusticism (which is the same as skoroborism), which are the olfactory, tactile, auditory, visual, and gustatory forms of sensory perception in skorism. Similar constructions are used, mutatis mutandis, in relation to hyloidism, which is neoscatistic, and its two main subdivisions, viz. hydroidism (whose central idiom is hydrism) and stereoidism (whose central idiom is stereism); hence, to avoid repetition, no reference will be made to hyloidaestheticism (comprising hydroidaestheticism and stereoidaestheticism) when we deal with hyloidism later.

Phthorism—culturally and individually one of the most important idioms at the phobophronesic level—is the idiom of destructiveness (destructiveness as an end in itself). Phthorophilia may be active (pragmophthorophilia or sadism) or passive (apragmophthorophilia or masochism); a third, very important, form is that of autophthorophilia (self-destructiveness). Autophthorophilia may be concrete (or practical), e.g. in those young men who go to the woods to gag themselves and tie themselves up etc., or it may be ideal, largely manifested by depression, apathy (in very severe cases), hypochondria, and a tendency to suicide (though suicide itself is, of course, a practical manifestation). Ideal autophthorophilia may be either impulsive (propetautophthorophilia, in which autophthorophilia is associated with propetophilia), or persistent (synechautophthorophilia). Synechautophthorophilia occurs in association with deutoscatism and we therefore treat it as a deutoscatistic condition, or, because of its palaeoscatistic content, as a pseudodeutoscatistic (more precisely a pseudohyperprotophasic) condition. Synechautophthorophilia is by far the most important form of autophthorophilia: we shall deal with it more fully later under deutoscatism. The term 'autophthorophilia' without qualification usually refers to synechautophthorophilia.

On the erotic side, phthorolagnia comprises pragmophthorolagnia (erotic sadism), apragmophthorolagnia (erotic masochism), and autophthorolagnia. On the cosmophobic side, phthorophobia (timidity) presents in a large variety of forms, including an erotic form (erotic phthorophobia or phthorolagnophobia) which in some cases may be specifically related to the genitals (genital-erotic phthorophobia or genital phthorolagnophobia).

Propetism (lack of control, or impulsiveness) is closely related to phthorism. There are four main forms of propetism: excretory (propetoskoreticism, comprising propetocopreticism ('encopresis') and propetureticism ('enuresis')), erotic (propetolagnia or propetorgastia), practical (impulsiveness), and ideal (instability). Impulsiveness should not be confused with uninhibitedness, which is a philophilic idiom. Ideal propetophilia frequently occurs in different combinations with idioms of phthorism and with other idioms of propetism in what we call propeto-phthorism. Finally, propetophobia is manifested as excessive inhibition.

Shame is a cosmophobic idiom; its hedonic equivalent is sadistic pride (or, simply, pride). Shame applies mainly in relation to excretion and in relation to eroticism that is conceived in sadistic and excretory terms (the sadistic-excretory (or palaeotropolagnic) concept of eroticism, or simply palaeotropolagnia). According to the sadistic-excretory concept, eroticism in general, and coitus in particular, is a sadistic and excretory act in which the man excretes his semen (or 'seminal excrement') inside the woman's vagina (hence the concept of the 'cesspit vagina'). Thus the sadistic-excretory concept of eroticism associates the penetrative-

1. A Synopsis of the Cosmophobia Theory

active role in coitus with sadistic pride and the receptive-passive role with shame or 'dishonour' (what we call androphobic shame, androlagnophobia, or, simply, androphobia).

Shame accounts for such cosmophobic taboos as those prohibiting excretory and erotic acts in public, as well as nudity (especially the exposure of the genitals) and other matters that have a bearing on 'obscenity' or 'indecency'.

It is common for shame to be combined with three other cosmophobic idioms (viz. scopophobia (shyness), phthorophobia (timidity), and propetophobia (excessive inhibition)) in what we call tetraphobia. Tetraphobia is mainly of clinical importance though it also has its cultural aspects, e.g. in its greater prevalence in women at the phobophronesic level of civilization.

26. Neoscatism represents the rest of scatism, which corresponds to a higher level of awareness than that of phagism. Neoscatism comprises deutoscatism, i.e. the deutoscatistic cycle and its idioms, and protoscatism, which represents the rest of neoscatism. In other words, protoscatism represents the whole of scatism excluding palaeoscatism at one end and deutoscatism at the other.

In neoscatism, unlike palaeoscatism, excreta are of value in an ideal sense, mainly as hydroids (water and its equivalents) and stereoids (solid matter and its equivalents). Hydroids and stereoids together constitute hyloids.

Some scatistic idioms are general scatistic idioms: they apply to more than one, or more or less to all three, of the three main divisions of scatism, viz. palaeoscatism, protoscatism, and deutoscatism. We have to study these idioms under one or another of the three main forms of phronesic orientation in scatism. Thus the idiom of rich phantasy and dream life will be dealt with under protoscatism, while the idioms of pessimism, personal independence, and hoarding will be dealt with under deutoscatism.

Deutoscatistic idioms, unlike both palaeoscatistic and protoscatistic idioms, have no cosmophobic forms and no erotic forms. The erotic forms of scatistic idioms are all dysphronesic and are referred to collectively as scatolagnia. Thus scatolagnia in its usual sense comprises palaeoscatolagnia and protoscatolagnia.

The main idioms of protoscatism are: skoreticism, holistic hyloidism (comprising hydroidism and stereoidism in their holistic forms), somateidism, and aestheticism. In addition, as noted before, in this monographic series we shall deal with rich phantasy and dream life under protoscatism (though we need not say any more about this idiom in the present account).

27. Skoreticism is a neoscatistic idiom representing pleasure and fear in relation to one's own excretory acts, viz. in relation to urination (ureticism) and defaecation (copreticism). Skoreticophilia includes normal pleasure in retaining excreta until they can be evacuated; we refer to this as ischoskoreticophilia, which comprises ischureticophilia and ischocopreticophilia. Skoreticophilia is dysphronesic if it is excessive (hyperskoreticophilia), as in patients who abuse diuretics or laxatives to augment their excretory pleasures; if it is erotic (skoreticolagnia); or if it is precipitate or premature (propetoskoreticophilia). Of course the cosmophobic forms of all skoreticistic idioms are dysphronesic.

Hyloidism is a neoscatistic idiom comprising hydroidism, i.e. love and fear of water and its equivalents, and stereoidism, i.e. love and fear of solid matter and its equivalents. Hyloidism may be protoscatistic or deutoscatistic. Protoscatistic hyloidism is holistic; it has hedonic and cosmophobic forms, the hedonic forms

Cosmophobia Theory Monographs

being potentially artistic. By contrast, deutoscatistic hyloidism is analytic (or, more fully, analytic-synthetic) and is entirely hedonic, hence we refer to it as analytic hyloidophilia (or, more fully, analytic-synthetic hyloidophilia). Analytic hyloidophilia, which is potentially scientific, comprises not only analytic hydroidophilia and analytic stereoidophilia but also a third, ideal form (ideal hyloidophilia or ideophilia).

The main idioms of holistic hydroidism, i.e. protoscatistic hydroidism, are: hydrism (water), pyrism (fire), aethrism (open space), hypsism (height), kinetism (movement), photism (light), thermism (heat), and aerism (air). In addition there are those idioms that hydroidism shares with mastosemeism, viz. leiism, malakism, leukism (viz. hydroleukism, as distinct from the mastoleukism of mastosemeism), and (indirectly) sphericism. Hydroidism also shares two idioms with somateidism, viz. entohydrism and emprosthism, to which we shall refer later. Finally, hydroidism also includes hydrochromatism (colour), comprising the colours of water and its ultimate prototype, viz. urine. Thus hydrochromatism comprises white (leukism, more precisely hydroleukism, as distinct from mastoleukism), yellow (xanthism), blue (cyanism), light grey or silver-grey (glaukism), colourless transparency (hyalism), and glistening (stilbism).

The main idioms of holistic stereoidism, i.e. protoscatistic stereoidism, are: stereism (solid matter), sclerism (hardness), xestism (smoothness in association with hardness, as distinct from smoothness in association with softness (leiism)), trachyism (roughness of surface), mesostereism (the amorphic, rugged interior of solid matter, in contrast to the smooth exterior (xestism)), apsophism (silence or stillness), brontism (explosives and explosive and other discontinuous sounds), entostereism (enclosed space), eremism (deserted places), scotism (darkness), and stereochromatism. Stereochromatism comprises the colour range yellow (xanthism, which is shared with hydrochromatism), orange, red (erythrism, which is shared with hysterosemeistic enterythrism), brown, and black (melanism, which is shared with phallosemeism). Stereoidism shares the following idioms with phallosemeism: sclerism, xestism, and oxyism. Stereoidism shares two idioms with somateidism: entostereism and opisthism. Finally, palaeism is an idiom of stereoidism that is sometimes seen in association with stereism; it represents the love and dislike of old objects, ranging from the preference of wearing old clothes to interest in archaeology.

28. Somateidism is a neoscatistic idiom representing concrete and ideal interest in, and fear of, human body-image, conceived in terms of one's own body. The emphasis on 'one's own body' in this definition has important sexual implications. Of course ever since the rise of civilization from savagery there has been a tendency in everything that is man-made to reflect the image of the human body, which is essentially bilaterally symmetrical but with a contrasting front and back. Thus the interest in body-image is very ancient in human mental evolution, but it is only in scatism, with its autotropia, that body-image acquires sufficient importance to be recognized as an independent idiom.

The main idioms of somateidism are: symmetrism, antitheticism, emprosthism and opisthism, entohydrism and entostereism, homaedeism, and monanalysis (monanalyticophilia). The idioms of symmetrism and antitheticism, manifested in a concrete or ideal form, arise from the bilateral symmetry and antero-posterior (or front-back) contrast of the human body, respectively. Moreover, the front and

1. A Synopsis of the Cosmophobia Theory

back of objects may each arouse interest or dislike or even fear, to which we refer as emprosthism and opisthism, respectively. It will be noted that the front of the human body is related to the urinary function while the back is similarly related to the defaecatory function. Hence the close relation between emprosthism and hydroidism, not only with love and fear of hydroids but also, more specifically and more concretely, with love and fear of penetrating, or being inside, water (entohydrism), e.g. in diving, including deep-sea diving, and (in a mechanized manner, the equivalent of flying in aeroplanes in the case of hypsism) in the interest and fear of submarines. Similarly, opisthism tends to be closely related to stereoidism, the equivalent of entohydrism being entostereism. As noted before, emprosthism and entohydrism are two idioms which hydroidism shares with somateidism; similarly, stereoidism shares opisthism and entostereism with somateidism. (However, emprosthism and opisthism are more closely related to somateidism than to hyloidism, whereas entohydrism and entostereism are more closely related to hyloidism than to somateidism.)

Entostereism, entohydrism, and hysterosemeism are sometimes collectively referred to as <u>entokoilism</u>.

Somateidism in relation to the individual's own genital configuration gives rise to the idiom of homaedeism, viz. homophallism in men and homohysterism in women. Homophallophilia and homohysterophilia are euphronesic, unless they are excessive; in the latter case (hyperhomaedeophilia: hyperhomophallophilia and hyperhomohysterophilia) they are usually associated not only with the erotic forms (viz. homophallolagnia and homohysterolagnia) but also with homolagnia (which is primarily a manifestation of general autolagnia).

Finally, monanalysis (monanalyticophilia) is a somateidophilic idiom representing pleasure in reducing things in a certain sphere to a single principle (as distinct from reducing them to two contrasting principles (dianalysis), which is a much more ancient manifestation of the human mind, as in the contrasting dualities of soul and body, mind and matter, etc.). Monanalysis arises from the desire to trace urine and faeces, in the ideal entokoilopragmoscopophilic sense, to their ultimate common origin as food in the mouth.

<u>Aestheticism</u> is the neoscatistic idiom representing pleasure and fear in relation to sensory perception. It includes hyloidaestheticism, viz. hydroidaestheticism and stereoidaestheticism, which is neoscatistic, but excludes skoroidaestheticism, viz. uroidaestheticism and coproidaestheticism, which is palaeoscatistic.

Of course sensory perception is important to man at all levels of civilization— and, on the biological level, is important to animals too. But it is only in scatism, because of its autotropia, that it acquires special importance, though this importance is very different in palaeoscatism and neoscatism, hence the use of different terms, viz. skoroidaestheticism in the case of skoroidism and aestheticism in the case of neoscatism.

Aestheticism comprises scopism (vision), hapticism (touch), acousticism (hearing), osphreticism (smell), and myotonism (the proprioceptive muscle sense). Scopophilia may be active (pragmoscopophilia), i.e. pleasure in seeing, or passive (apragmoscopophilia or exhibitionism), i.e. pleasure in being seen. Scopophobia generally represents the fear of being seen or observed, but occasionally it may occur in relation to seeing or observing.

Pragmoscopophilia in an ideal form is of basic importance in the process of thinking: in thinking we 'see' things with our minds.

Terminology is different in the case of the erotic forms of aestheticism. 'Aestheticolagnia' is the term for normal (i.e. euphronesic) sensory perception in eroticism, the scatolagnic forms of aestheticism being referred to as hyperaestheticolagnia (hyperscopolagnia, hyperhapticolagnia, etc.).

29. Deutoscatism is based on the deutoscatistic cycle, which is largely an ideal cycle representing the reflection in awareness of a physical (or biological) cycle of faecal retentiveness (though the term 'deutoscatistic cycle' is sometimes also applied to the biological prototype). This biological cycle consists of three phases: a prolonged phase of faecal retention, followed by a much shorter but intense phase of thorough faecal evacuation which serves as a prelude to the third phase, which is one of sociability after the greater or lesser solitude of the first two phases. The reflection in awareness of these three phases, which together form the deutoscatistic cycle, are referred to, respectively, as the protophase, or first deutoscatistic phase, which is one of relative inactivity or brooding; the deutophase, or second deutoscatistic phase or 'metamorphic phase', which is one of intense activity; and the tritophase, or third deutoscatistic phase, which is essentially a phagistic, mainly philophilic, phase. In the protophase and deutophase, deutohedonia (i.e. scatohedonia) predominates, but it gives way to protohedonia (i.e. phagohedonia) in the tritophase: the tritophase is largely represented by sociability (i.e. interest in people, or love in the idiophilic sense), food, and eroticism (the latter, as noted before, is essentially a special form of idiophilia).

Deutoscatistic idioms may be either protophasic or deutophasic; there are no tritophasic idioms as these are merely those of philism (and other forms of phagism as well as eroticism which is derived from idiophilia). In addition, as noted before, we shall, for convenience, deal with three general scatistic idioms under deutoscatism, viz. pessimism, personal independence, and hoarding. Protophasic idioms comprise: patience (cartericophilia), encratophilia (self-restraint), pragmatophilia (practicality), procrastination, and synnoophilia (sustained thought). Deutophasic idioms comprise: ergophilia (intensive work), catharophilia (cleanliness), taxiphilia (orderliness), teleophilia (perfectionism), monosynthesis (monosyntheticophilia), metamorphophilia, analytic hyloidophilia, and aeoniophilia. In addition, there are two major dysphronesic idioms, viz. sphalerohedonia and autophthorophilia, which are both due to the indefinite prolongation of the protophase (hyperprotophasia). Before we briefly discuss some of these idioms— we have already dealt with analytic hyloidophilia—it is important to note that, in individuals and cultures, it is common to see a predominance of either the protophase or the deutophase; hence we often speak of polyprotophasia and polydeutophasia. As the deutophase serves as a prelude to the tritophase, polydeutophasia also implies relative polytritophasia, i.e. relative (though only relative) polyphilia, which may amount to philophilio-deutoscatism; and vice versa: polyprotophasia is generally associated with oligophilia. In some cases there is a tendency for both the protophase and the deutophase to be pronounced while each of them lasts (the tritophase, as always, being closely associated with the deutophase which, as noted before, serves as a prelude to it). We refer to the tendency to oscillate between marked protophasia and marked deutophasia as aeolophasia. Pathologically excessive aeolophasia (hyperaeolophasia) may complicate amphiphilia, in which case the aphilic phase of amphiphilia will be complicated by hyperprotophasia (in the form of sphalerohedonia and/or autophthorophilia) while the hyperphilic phase of amphiphilia will be complicated by hyperdeutophasia (e.g. in the form of hyperergophilia).

Pessimism is characteristic of scatism because scatism, which is based on the excretory functions, is essentially a reaction to a world of scarcity and adversity, whereas phagism, which is based on the alimentary function, is essentially a reaction to a favourable world of abundance (hence the philophilic idiom of optimism). Personal independence is a collective term for the desire to have one's own way; it comprises four idioms (or a certain aspect of them): autotropia (a general scatistic idiom), stubbornness (which combines autotropia with sadism or propetophthorism), self-willedness (a general deutoscatistic idiom, i.e. not limited to any one phase), and individualism (a postphobophronesic idiom, the opposite of prephobophronesic collectivism). Hoarding is a general scatistic idiom that comprises hoarding proper, in relation to objects of protohedonic value, and collecting, in relation to objects of deutohedonic value.

Metamorphophilia is of immense importance as a deutophasic idiom, and largely underlies the other deutophasic idioms, hence the reference to the deutophase as the metamorphic phase and to its idioms as the metamorphic idioms. For metamorphophilia represents pleasure in transforming the quality or nature of things, as by transforming the worthless into the valuable in teleophilia, the chaotic into the orderly in taxiphilia, and the dirty into the clean in catharophilia. Moreover, it will be noted that such transformations not only imply a creative element but also imply transforming the natural into the artificial or man-made. We refer to this latter factor as artificialism or anthropopoietophilia, in contrast to the naturalism or autophyophilia that characterizes both phagohedonia and protoscatohedonia.

30. Next we consider the two clinically important pathological idioms of deutoscatism: sphalerohedonia (precarious hedonia) and autophthorophilia (self-destructiveness). In sphalerohedonia (the 'obsessional neurosis' of descriptive psychiatry), on a phagobasis of aphilia the protohedonia of the tritophase becomes precarious (due, of course, to genetic factors), i.e. there is a threat of the tritophase never materializing. This leads to an enforced, indefinite prolongation of the protophase (hyperprotophasia) in an attempt to substitute deutohedonia for protohedonia for as long as the protohedonia of the tritophase remains uncertain. Sphalerohedonic hyperprotophasia is usually characterized by two main pathological idioms: hypersynnoophilia and enantioscatism. Thus the indefinite prolongation of the protophase results in a state of mental stagnation (hypersynnoophilia), i.e. a state in which thought goes round and round without reaching its normal conclusion, like an engine idling in neutral gear. This state of mental stagnation is manifested clinically by the phenomenon of 'obsession', i.e. of interminable thoughts, doubts, etc. which the patient desperately wants to bring to a conclusion. Hypersynnoophilia may also present as a state superficially resembling the prephobosymphronesia of the savage (pseudosymphronesia), usually taking the form of pseudomagic, mainly the belief in omens and rituals which is used in the attempt to bring the enforced hyperprotophasia to an end. In a different way, the precarious hedonia of the tritophase, resting on a phagobasis of aphilia, may provoke a palaeoscatistic reaction, viz. dyshedonic tendencies such as those of sadism, including antiphobic sadism, coprophilia, mysophilia, and propetophilia, conflicting with their cosmophobic equivalents, especially moral phthorophobia—a conflict to which we refer as

enantioscatism. Though usually the exaggerated moral phthorophobia keeps the dyshedonic tendencies under control, the conflict may cause the patient great distress.

Autophthorophilia—the 'endogenous depression' or 'psychotic depression' of descriptive psychiatry—is another pathological scatistic idiom that rests on a phagobasis of aphilia. It has two forms, impulsive (propetautophthorophilia) and persistent (synechautophthorophilia). The latter is by far the more important clinically, hence the inclusion of the condition under deutoscatism (which of course does not apply to propetautophthorophilia), and hence the fact that 'autophthorophilia' unqualified generally means synechautophthorophilia. The condition is mainly ideal, though practical autophthorophilia is evident in the act of suicide. Often the autophthorophilia is partly moral (moral autophthorophilia), giving rise to the familiar delusions of guilt and unworthiness, self-accusatory delusions, etc. (However, these delusions represent extreme moral autophthorophilia which is regarded as pathological even by phobophronesic standards: milder moral autophthorophilia, without full-blown autophthorophilia, is 'normal' at the phobophronesic level of civilization.) The hypochondria which is a common feature of the disease—ranging from the belief that one's body is being eaten away by cancer or some other sinister disease to the highly significant complaint of 'blockage of the bowels'—is the direct product of the autophthorophilia. It is worth noting that autophthorophilia—which, strictly speaking, is a hedonic, more precisely a dyshedonic, condition—is in reality an anhedonic (or anhedonizing) condition: it substitutes the self-destructive dyshedonia of autophthorophilia for the will to live of normal hedonia. The clinical picture depends on the balance between the autophthorophilia and residual normal hedonia (i.e. life-loving hedonia). Hence there may be conflicting symptoms in the same patient at the same time. For example, the very patient who has a marked suicidal inclination may be afraid of dying, and may indeed be unable to go to sleep at night for fear of dying (as if by keeping awake he could ward off death).

Finally, the close relation between autophthorophilia and sphalerohedonia should be noted. Both conditions rest on a phagobasis of aphilia, and both represent an indefinite prolongation of the protophase (hyperprotophasia). However, the prolongation is enforced in sphalerohedonia but not in autophthorophilia, i.e. in sphalerohedonia the prolongation of the protophase is forced on the patient because of his uncertainty about the protohedonia of the tritophase, but in autophthorophilia the prolongation is not enforced: the patient (in so far as autophthorophilia itself is concerned, as distinct from residual normal hedonia) has no use for the tritophase: his aphilia has led, not to precarious protohedonia as in sphalerohedonia, but to protohedonic loss to which he has reacted with self-destructiveness so that he may relish suicide with the same gusto with which normal people enjoy life. It will be noted that in the hyperprotophasia that underlies both sphalerohedonia and autophthorophilia (i.e. synechautophthorophilia), the indefinitely prolonged protophase—though occurring in a deutoscatist and belonging to the deutoscatistic cycle—has a largely palaeoscatistic content (viz. enantioscatism in the case of sphalerohedonia, and the autophthorophilia itself in the case of autophthorophilia). Hence hyperprotophasia to a great extent (more in autophthorophilia than in sphalerohedonia) represents pseudohyperprotophasia. (Hypersynnoophilia is deutoscatistic and not palaeoscatistic: it occurs in both conditions but is incomparably more important in sphalerohedonia because of the enforced nature of hyperprotophasia in it.)

Chapter 5

EROTICISM

31. Eroticism is the reflection in awareness of the genital function whose very essence in man (as in other mammals) is the penetration of the female by the male in the act of coitus—an act which we describe as being pregnancy-like, quasi-conceptive, or kyesioid, because in it the woman contains the male penis in her genital tract (or 'womb', as the term is used in the psychogenetic sense) in much the same way as she contains the unborn child in pregnancy. Hence if all hedonia, whose prototype is idiophilia, ultimately represents metrophilia (= mother-love) or metropalinodophilia (= mother-reunion love), eroticism represents erotic idiophilia, ultimately kyemetrophilia (= kyesioid mother-love) or kyemetropalinodophilia (= kyesioid mother-reunion love). Thus eroticism is a special form of idiophilia which is characterized (under the influence of the biological sexual instinct) by being normally limited to the opposite sex, by being concrete (or practical), i.e. by being typically expressed in physical (or bodily) action (unlike idiophilia proper, which is mainly ideal), and by this physical action representing in an endless variety of forms (in the different forms of precoital loveplay as well as in coitus itself) this basic element of quasi-conceptive penetration or containment. This quasi-conceptive element of penetration is also the basis of dyseroticism, i.e. pathological eroticism, which (with a few exceptions, e.g. hypereroticism) differs from eueroticism, i.e. normal eroticism, in not—actually or potentially—serving the function of reproduction. In other words, normal heterolagnic coitus between a man and a woman, whose essence is the penetration of the vagina by the penis, is the prototype of all eroticism, both normal and pathological. That normal coitus between a man and a woman is the primary model of all eroticism is evident not only from the fact that in homolagnia in both sexes the patients imitate normal coitus and even assign a 'man's role' and a 'woman's role' in their relationships, but also from the fact that in autolagnia proper in both sexes the patients frequently attempt self-coitus as best they can—indeed the hand-genital relation in masturbation may be seen as ultimately representing self-coitus, the hand playing a receptive, 'feminine' role in relation to the penis in male masturbation, and a (potentially or actually) penetrative, 'masculine' role in relation to the vulva in female masturbation.

These two basic roles that pervade all eroticism are more accurately described as the penetrative-active role and the receptive-passive role, or penetrative-active eroticism and receptive-passive eroticism. The activeness and passiveness ultimately represent active and passive preservative devouring (i.e. preservative devouring and devouredness), respectively. Because penetration is the central feature of eroticism, the (active and passive) preservative devouring is most characteristically, though by no means exclusively, internal. By internal devouring (as distinct from external devouring, which is the ordinary form of devouring) we mean devouring from inside.

We speak of female penetrability or hysteroid penetrability with reference to the woman being doubly penetrable: coital penetrability and gestational penetrability denote the woman's containment in her womb ('womb' in the psychogenetic sense of the female genital tract) of the penis in coitus and of the child in pregnancy, respectively. The main difference between the two is the great power of active internal (preservative) devouring possessed by the penis, whereas the child in utero is passively (preservatively) devoured by his or her mother.

32. Dyseroticism arises from three main causes: cosmophobia, aphilia, and autolagnia. Cosmophobic eroticism is referred to collectively as erotophobia. This includes aphormic sexual cosmophobia, androphobia (especially in women), shame (other than androphobia), tetraphobic erotophobia, and aetherotophobia. Aphilic dyseroticism is generally the cause of the milder, and commoner, forms of dyseroticism. It includes hyperphilic hypereroticism, as hyperphilia is a derivative of aphilia. Autolagnic dyseroticism, or simply autolagnia (or auteroticism), i.e. erotic self-love, is the cause of the more serious forms of dyseroticism, and is inherently associated with hypereroticism (autolagnic hypereroticism) which differs considerably from hyperphilic hypereroticism. Autolagnia has two main forms: general autolagnia and scatolagnia. General autolagnia comprises autolagnia proper, homolagnia or homeroticism (erotic attraction to members of one's own sex, as against the normal attraction to members of the opposite sex), and reversed heterolagnia (viz. passive male heterolagnia in men and active female heterolagnia in women). Scatolagnia is a collective term for the erotic forms of scatistic idioms, e.g. hydrolagnia, pyrolagnia, aethrolagnia, and phthorolagnia in all its forms. Scatolagnia cannot occur without general autolagnia, but general autolagnia may occur without any scatolagnia. It is important to note that euereoticism rests on a phagobasis of idiophilia (hence we have described it as erotic idiophilia or a special form of idiophilia), but autolagnia rests on a basis of autophilia, which is scatistic. This is true of autolagnia whether it presents in a completely autolagnic or in a homolagnic or in a heterolagnic setting. For example, an autolagnic condition (such as erotic sadism or leather or rubber dyslagnia) is basically autolagnic whether it presents in a completely autolagnic or in a homolagnic or heterolagnic setting.

Although all forms of dyseroticism have their sociological (or cultural) and clinical (or individual) forms, erotophobia is on the whole more important culturally than individually, while the aphilic and autolagnic forms of dyseroticism are more important individually than culturally.

33. Closely related to the concept of eroticism as kyemetrophilia is that of eroticism as organophoria. Using 'exo-' for 'external', 'endo-' for 'internal', and '-phore' for 'bearing', we may say that men are exophallophores, whereas women are exomastophores and endopaedophores and, in coitus, endophallophores. The list is not complete but it will suffice to point out the equivalence of the three 'organs': the penis, the breast, and the child.

34. Apart from the kyemetrophilic concept of eroticism, which is universal at the diaphronesic (both phobophronesic and postphobophronesic) level, and which is essentially euphronesic, there is the sadistic-excretory concept of eroticism, or the palaeotropolagnic concept of eroticism or (simply) palaeotropolagnia, which is a wholly phobophronesic concept that equates coitus with an excretory act in which the man deposits his seminal excrement (= the semen conceived as excrement) inside the woman's vagina (cesspit vagina). This is the basis of the familiar concept

of coitus as a triumph and a source of sadistic pride for the man, but as a defilement and a source of shame and 'dishonour' for the woman. We refer to shame in relation to the receptive-passive role in coitus in particular, and in eroticism in general, as <u>androphobic shame</u>, or simply as <u>androphobia</u> (= androlagnophobia). Androphobia has far-reaching sociological and clinical implications. It was a major factor in depriving women of all erotic rights: they had to be 'pure' virgins until they married, and had to remain 'chaste' after marriage. An 'unchaste' woman, i.e. one 'dishonoured' by coitus with a man other than her husband, was murdered by her male relatives, who were 'dishonoured' by her 'dishonour'. Androphobia used to be a major cause of anancosymphronesia in clinical practice in civilized society—and it still is in countries where women remain unliberated.

35. Next we deal with <u>organolagnia</u> or <u>organ-eroticism</u>, i.e. the experience of erotic pleasure in relation to a specific organ (i.e. part) of the body. The organ concerned may be in the subject's own body (<u>endorganolagnia</u> or <u>enderoticism</u> or <u>subject-eroticism</u>) or in the erotic object's body (<u>exorganolagnia</u> or <u>exeroticism</u> or <u>object-eroticism</u>). <u>Allelorganolagnia</u> denotes erotic pleasure involving two specified organs, typically one organ in each of two individuals of the opposite or of the same sex, but in the case of autolagnia (always distinguished by the prefix 'auto-') the two organs are in the subject's own body. For example, the phallovaginal relation in normal coitus may be described as phallocolpolagnia (= penis-vagina eroticism) or as allelaedeolagnia (= genital-to-genital, or bigenital, eroticism), and mouth-to-mouth kissing may be described as allelostomatolagnia, while the commonest form of masturbation in men is that of autocheirophallolagnia (= self-hand-penis eroticism). <u>Erotopoeicity</u> is the capacity of an organ or of an inanimate object to give erotic pleasure. In the case of an organ, the erotopoeicity may be in the form of either <u>enderotopoeicity</u> or <u>exerotopoeicity</u>, depending on whether the pleasure is enderotic or exerotic, respectively. In all organolagnia the exerotic form may be, in one sense, regarded as the primary form inasmuch as all non-erotic hedonia, and also all eroticism in relation to inanimate objects, are of the object-form. <u>Erethopoeicity</u> is closely related to erotopoeicity, but the latter refers to erotic pleasure in the widest sense, which includes ideal eroticism (i.e. eroticism unassociated with the physical phenomena of erotic arousal, i.e. unassociated with <u>eroterethia</u> or, simply, <u>erethia</u>), whereas 'erethopoeicity' means specifically the capacity to give rise to eroterethia.

As for the classification of organolagnia, it will be noted that the prototype of eroticism, as of philism, is the oro-mammary relation of the lactivorous stage of life—the main difference being that philism is essentially ideal, whereas eroticism is concrete (or practical or physical). The oro-mammary relation forms the prototype of erotic penetration; i.e. the biological act of copulation is conceived in human awareness in terms of the ontogenetically earlier lactivorous stage of life. Thus there are two main foci for the development of organ-eroticism: the genital, which is directly derived from the biological genital function, and the oro-mammary (i.e. oral and mammary), which is derived from the eroticization in adulthood of the oro-mammary prototype in the lactivorous stage of life (the oro-mammary relation itself in the suckling infant is, of course, not erotic). We refer to eroticism of the genital organs as <u>aedeorganolagnia</u>, or simply as <u>aedeolagnia</u>, which comprises <u>andraedeolagnia</u> (eroticism of the male genitals) and <u>gynaedeolagnia</u> (eroticism of the female genitals). Erotic diffusion from the genital organs to most of the organs of the lower part of the body (the buttocks and thighs etc.) gives rise to paraedeorganolagnia, or simply paraedeolagnia. Aedeolagnia and paraedeolagnia together constitute periaedeorganolagnia. Similar considerations apply to the oro-mammary focus: stomatomastorganolagnia comprises eroticism of the mouth (stomatolagnia) and of the female breasts (mastolagnia). (The term should not be confused with 'stomatomastolagnia', which is a form of allelorganolagnia, viz. mouth-breast eroticism.) Parastomatomastorganolagnia comprises parastomatolagnia and paramastolagnia and, together with stomatomastorganolagnia, constitutes peristomatomastorganolagnia.

36. Sensory perception in eroticism is referred to as aestheticolagnia. Aestheticolagnia is an idiom of eroticism: it is not the erotic form of the scatistic idiom of aestheticism: the latter is represented by hyperaestheticolagnia (which is a form of scatolagnia). Aestheticolagnia comprises scopolagnia (viz. pragmoscopolagnia and apragmoscopolagnia (erotic exhibitionism)), hapticolagnia, acousticolagnia, osphreticolagnia, geusticolagnia, and myotonolagnia (including the myotonolagnia of the orgasm).

Chapter 6

SCHEME OF THE

COSMOPHOBIA THEORY MONOGRAPHS

37. The Cosmophobia Theory Monographs is a series of 67 monographs. The monographs are arranged in four main groups: Introduction, Phylopsychogenesis, Ontopsychogenesis, and Miscellaneous Monographs. The Introduction comprises only one monograph, viz. the present monograph (A Synopsis of the Cosmophobia Theory). The monographs on Phylopsychogenesis are subdivided into those on Prephobophronesia, on Phobophronesia, and on Postphobophronesia. The monographs on Ontopsychogenesis comprise those on Prephobophronesia (Palissymphronesia and Anancosymphronesia) and those numerous ones on Biophronesia (comprising one introductory monograph followed by those on Phagism, Palaeoscatism, Protoscatism, Deutoscatism, and Eroticism). Finally, the Miscellaneous Monographs include a Glossary and an Index.

It is hardly necessary to point out that in a theory that correlates sociology and psychiatry, the study of phylopsychogenesis and of ontopsychogenesis largely overlap. There are also practical considerations; for example, the psychogenetic study of art could not be undertaken until philophilia had been dealt with.

In the following table the 67 monographs are listed, giving in each case the monograph number and title abbreviation, followed by the short title of the monograph, and finally the full title. For example, in the entry '3.Rel Religion The Psychogenesis of Religion', '3' is the number of the monograph in the series of 67 monographs, 'Rel' is the title abbreviation used in the Index, while 'Religion' is the short title generally used in other monographs to refer to this particular monograph (i.e. the monograph is generally referred to as 'the monograph on Religion'); finally the full title of the monograph is given, viz. The Psychogenesis of Religion.

Cosmophobia Theory Monographs

COSMOPHOBIA THEORY MONOGRAPHS

INTRODUCTION

1.Syn	Synopsis	A Synopsis of the Cosmophobia Theory

PHYLOPSYCHOGENESIS

Prephobophronesia: The Stage of Savagery

2.Mag	Magic	The Psychogenesis of Magic
3.Rel	Religion	The Psychogenesis of Religion
4.Mge	Marriage	The Psychogenesis of Marriage
5.Gov	Government	The Psychogenesis of Government
6.Coll	Collectivism	The Psychogenesis of Collectivism and Totemism

Phobophronesia: The Stage of Civilization

7.Civ	Civilization	Civilization—Backward and Progressive
8.MA	Middle Ages	The Middle Ages: A study in psychogenesis

Postphobophronesia: The Future of Civilization

9.Ath	Atheism	Atheism and Rational Morality: The future of religion
10.Ag	Agamy	Agamy and Women's Liberation: The future of marriage
11.Ac	Acracy	Acracy and World Peace: The future of government
12.Sci	Science	Science, Philosophy, and Art: Towards a rational world civilization

ONTOPSYCHOGENESIS

Prephobophronesia

13.Pali	Palissymphronesia	Palissymphronesia
14.Ananc	Anancosymphronesia	Anancosymphronesia

Biophronesia

1. Introduction

15.Bio	Biophronesia	Biophronesia

2. Phagism

16.Phil	Philism	Philism
17.Geneo	Geneosemeia	Geneosemeia
18.Oral	Oral Concept	The Oral Concept of the World: A study in the origins of human thought
19.Art	Art	Art: A psychogenetic study
20.Sit	Sitism	Sitism
21.Hect	Hectism	Hectism

3. Palaeoscatism

22.Skoroid	Skoroidism	Skoroidism
23.Phth	Phthorism	Phthorism
24.Prop	Propetism	Propetism
25.Shame	Shame	Shame

1. A Synopsis of the Cosmophobia Theory

4. Protoscatism